I Can Subtract, It's Not an Act!

Tracy Kompelien

Consulting Editors, Diane Craig, M.A./Reading Specialist
and Susan Kosel, M.A. Education

Published by ABDO Publishing Company, 4940 Viking Drive, Edina, Minnesota 55435.

Printed in the United States.

Credits
Edited by: Pam Price
Curriculum Coordinator: Nancy Tuminelly
Cover and Interior Design and Production: Mighty Media
Photo Credits: Corbis Images, Photodisc, ShutterStock, Wewerka Photography

Library of Congress Cataloging-in-Publication Data

Kompelien, Tracy, 1975-
    I can subtract, it's not an act! / Tracy Kompelien
      p. cm. -- (Math made fun)
    ISBN 10 1-59928-523-1 (hardcover)
    ISBN 10 1-59928-524-X (paperback)

    ISBN 13 978-1-59928-523-8 (hardcover)
    ISBN 13 978-1-59928-524-5 (paperback)
    1. Subtraction--Juvenile literature. I. Title. II. Series.

QA115.K664 2007
513.2'12--dc22

                                         2006015301

SandCastle Level: Transitional

SandCastle™ books are created by a professional team of educators, reading specialists, and content developers around five essential components—phonemic awareness, phonics, vocabulary, text comprehension, and fluency—to assist young readers as they develop reading skills and strategies and increase their general knowledge. All books are written, reviewed, and leveled for guided reading, early reading intervention, and Accelerated Reader® programs for use in shared, guided, and independent reading and writing activities to support a balanced approach to literacy instruction. The SandCastle™ series has four levels that correspond to early literacy development. The levels help teachers and parents select appropriate books for young readers.

Emerging Readers
(no flags)

Beginning Readers
(1 flag)

Transitional Readers
(2 flags)

Fluent Readers
(3 flags)

These levels are meant only as a guide. All levels are subject to change.

To subtract

is to take something
away from another.

Words used to
describe subtracting:
count back
difference
minus
number line
take away

1 2 3 4 5 6 7 8 9 10

This is a number line. We are subtracting when we count back on the number line.

The ⬡ is on the 7.

I count back 3 places.

When I subtract 3

from 7, the difference is 4.

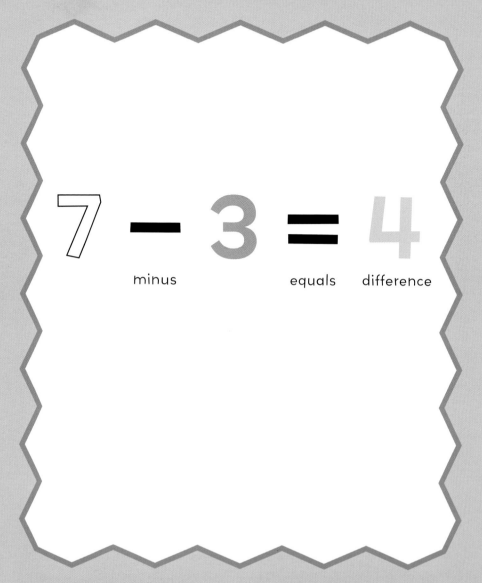

7 − 3 = 4

minus   equals   difference

I can show subtraction with a number sentence, or equation.

I know that when you subtract a part from a whole, you get the difference.

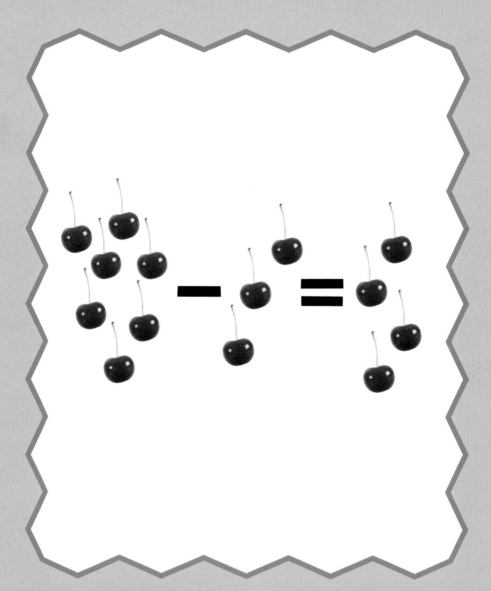

eight
8

I see that there are

7 cherries.

I take away 3 and

the difference is 4.

I Can Subtract, It's Not an Act!

There are 8 toys
on the floor.

John puts 5 on a shelf
by the  .

8 − 5 = 3

twelve
12

John puts 2 toys

on his ,

next to the 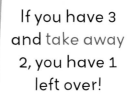 he

and his mom read.

If you have 3
and take away
2, you have 1
left over!

$3 - 2 = 1$

There is **1** left on the floor.

John puts it in a ,

and there are no more.

I Can Subtract Every Day!

Steph likes to eat crackers. She takes away 2 to eat.

$10 - 2 = 8$

Steph is still hungry.
This time she subtracts
4 crackers to eat.

$8 - 4 = 4$

twenty
20

Steph likes the round
crackers the most.
She takes away 2 more.

$4 - 2 = 2$

Can you find the difference of the crackers Steph started with and the crackers that are left?

If I started with 10 and have 2 left, how many did I eat?

$10 - 2 = 8$

Glossary

count back – to take away numbers one at a time.

difference – the answer to a subtraction problem.

number line – a line that is marked with a series of numbers.

subtract – to find the difference of two numbers by taking away part of the whole.

take away – to remove.

whole – in subtraction, the number you start with.